W9-BYX-929

SandCastle

What Should I Eat?

Grains
Are Good

Amanda Rondeau

Consulting Editor
Monica Marx, M.A./Reading Specialist

ABDO
Publishing Company

Published by SandCastle™, an imprint of ABDO Publishing Company, 4940 Viking Drive, Edina, Minnesota 55435.

Credits
Edited by: Pam Price
Curriculum Coordinator: Nancy Tuminelly
Cover and Interior Design and Production: Mighty Media
Photo Credits: Banana Stock, Brand X Pictures, Comstock, Corbis Images, Eyewire Images, Image Source, PhotoDisc, Thinkstock

Library of Congress Cataloging-in-Publication Data

Rondeau, Amanda, 1974-
    Grains are good / Amanda Rondeau.
       p. cm. -- (What should I eat?)
    Includes index.
    Summary: A simple introduction to the grain group of foods and why grains are important for us to eat.
       ISBN 1-57765-833-7
       1. Cereals as food--Juvenile literature. 2. Nutrition--Juvenile literature. [1. Grain. 2. Nutrition.] I. Title.

TX557 .R562 2002
641.3'31--dc21
                                                                                2002018364

SandCastle™ books are created by a professional team of educators, reading specialists, and content developers around five essential components that include phonemic awareness, phonics, vocabulary, text comprehension, and fluency. All books are written, reviewed, and leveled for guided reading, early intervention reading, and Accelerated Reader® programs and designed for use in shared, guided, and independent reading and writing activities to support a balanced approach to literacy instruction.

Let Us Know

After reading the book, SandCastle would like you to tell us your stories about reading. What is your favorite page? Was there something hard that you needed help with? Share the ups and downs of learning to read. We want to hear from you! To get posted on the ABDO Publishing Company Web site, send us email at:

sandcastle@abdopub.com

SandCastle Level: Transitional

What is the grain group?

Fats & Sweets — Eat LESS

MILK Group
2–3 servings

PROTEIN Group
2–3 servings

VEGETABLE Group
3–5 servings

FRUIT Group
2–4 servings

PEANUT BUTTER

FRUIT JUICE

GRAIN Group **6–11** servings

*For suggested serving sizes, see page 22.

This is the food pyramid.

There are 6 food groups in the pyramid.

The food pyramid helps us know how to eat right.

Eating right helps us stay healthy.

The grain group is part of the food pyramid.

We should eat 6 to 11 servings from the grain group every day.

Foods in the grain group are good for our bodies.

There are many kinds of grains in the grain group.

Foods in the grain group give us the energy that we need.

Grains help us stay strong.

Did you know pasta
is a grain?

Pasta is usually made
with wheat.

Pasta is good plain or with
tomato sauce for lunch
or dinner.

Did you know cereal is a grain?

Cereal is made from lots of grains, like rice, corn, and wheat.

Cereal is good hot or cold for breakfast.

Did you know bread
is a grain?

There are more than
1,000 kinds of bread.

Some kinds of bread are
bagels, rolls, and loaves.

Bread is great for
sandwiches.

Did you know rice
is a grain?

Many people in other
countries eat rice
3 times a day.

Rice is great with
vegetables for dinner.

Can you think of other foods in the grain group?

What is your favorite food in the grain group?

Index

What Counts As a Serving?

Bread, Cereal, Rice, and Pasta		
1 slice of bread	1 ounce of ready-to-eat cereal	½ cup of cooked cereal, rice, or pasta

Glossary

breakfast   the first meal after you wake up in the morning

country   a nation with its own government

food pyramid   a guide to healthy eating

grain   the seed of cereal plants, like rice and wheat

healthy   to be well, also doing things that keep us well

loaf   bread baked in one large piece

serving   a single portion of food

wheat   a cereal grass grown for its seed

About SandCastle™

A professional team of educators, reading specialists, and content developers created the SandCastle™ series to support young readers as they develop reading skills and strategies and increase their general knowledge. The SandCastle™ series has four levels that correspond to early literacy development in young children. The levels are provided to help teachers and parents select the appropriate books for young readers.

Emerging Readers
(no flags)

Beginning Readers
(1 flag)

Transitional Readers
(2 flags)

Fluent Readers
(3 flags)

These levels are meant only as a guide. All levels are subject to change.

To see a complete list of SandCastle™ books and other nonfiction titles from ABDO Publishing Company, visit www.abdopub.com or contact us at:

4940 Viking Drive, Edina, Minnesota 55435 • 1-800-800-1312 • fax: 1-952-831-1632